A Girl's Guide

Makeup and Skin Care

Caroline Curvan

ELDORADO INK

Eldorado Ink
PO Box 100097
Pittsburgh, PA 15233
www.eldoradoink.com

Produced by OTTN Publishing, Stockton, New Jersey

CPSIA compliance information: Batch#GG2017.
For further information, contact Eldorado Ink at info@eldoradoink.com.

First printing

1 3 5 7 9 8 6 4 2

Library of Congress Cataloging-in-Publication Data

on file at the Library of Congress
ISBN 978-1-61900-108-4 (hc)
ISBN 978-1-61900-116-9 (ebook)

About the Author: Caroline Curvan has worked behind the scenes on Broadway musicals featuring ancient Egyptians, 1930s murderesses, drag queens and more. When not in the theatre, she runs marathons, writes novels and teaches college English courses. Her favorite cosmetic is glitter.

Photo Credits: used under license from Shutterstock, Inc.: 1, 4, 6, 7, 10, 11, 13, 14, 16, 20, 23, 24, 25, 26, 27, 28, 29, 30, 31, 32, 33, 34, 35, 36, 37, 38, 40, 42, cover; Helga Esteb / Shutterstock.com: 18; D. Free / Shutterstock.com: 19 (top left; top right; bottom right); Jaguar PS / Shutterstock.com: 19 (top center); Niloo / Shutterstock.com: 9; Tinseltown / Shutterstock.com: 19 (bottom left).

For information about custom editions, special sales, or premiums, please contact our special sales department at info@eldoradoink.com.

Table of Contents

Skin Care Basics

You want to wear makeup, but where to start? With all the choices out there, it can be a tricky world to navigate. What to use? How to choose? Where to buy it? How to apply it? What's on trend and does that matter?

This book will help point you in the right direction to learn the basics so you can experiment, have fun, and enhance your natural beauty.

Thanks to the Internet, advice of all kinds is available. From YouTube videos to online questionnaires to Instagram, it can all be confusing and even contradictory. This book will also help you sift through the chatter and figure out what's right for you.

It's important to keep in mind that makeup is simply a tool to help you present your best face to the world, not to look like someone else. Practicing a minimalist approach will help enhance your natural features, give you a healthy, well-rested look and maybe even loan you a shot of confidence to navigate the sometimes crazy world of middle and high school.

GETTING STARTED

First and foremost, if you want your face to look good, you have to begin with your skin. Your skin is your canvas and you want to start with a smooth, healthy surface.

Teen years are tough, as your hormones fluctuate and your body produces lots of excess oil. Combine this with sports, stress, a less-than-perfect diet, and lack of sleep, you can find yourself looking tired and run down, with breakouts, blackheads, and acne. For that clean, dewy fresh look, you want to develop a simple routine that you can stick to.

First, if you have serious issues with acne, consult a dermatologist. These doctors specialize in skin problems and can help identify and correct problems before they become big issues. They will also give you advice on caring for your particular type of skin.

Whether or not you have acne, it's important to wash your face twice a day to remove dirt, excess oil, and dead skin.

WHAT TYPE OF SKIN DO YOU HAVE?

How you care for your skin depends on what type of skin you have. In order to clean your face properly, it's essential to know what you're dealing with. Try this test to determine your skin type:

1. Wash your face before bed using a gentle cleanser. Don't use any moisturizer after cleansing.

2. In the morning, assess how your skin feels and look at it closely in the mirror. Then dab your face with a tissue.

What do you see? Is your skin:

*   Dry and tight? Do you even see little flakes of dead skin here and there? If so, then you probably have Dry Skin.

*   Do you see grease on the tissue? An oily sheen on your face? If so, then you probably have Oily Skin.

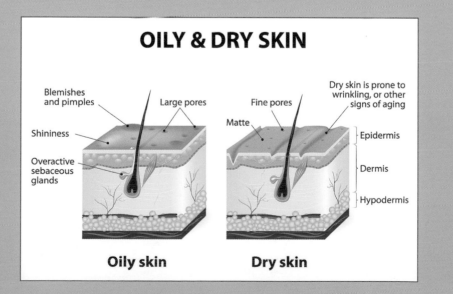

OILY & DRY SKIN

Blemishes and pimples
Large pores
Shininess
Overactive sebaceous glands

Fine pores
Matte
Dry skin is prone to wrinkling, or other signs of aging
Epidermis
Dermis
Hypodermis

Oily skin   **Dry skin**

- Do you see grease on the tissue when you blot some places but not others? Maybe you see dry, flaky patches here and there? If so, then you probably have Combination Skin, the most common skin type. Usually skin is oily in the "T-zone" (chin, nose, and forehead area) and normal to dry everywhere else.

- Does your skin look irritated or blotchy? Or, in the past, have you noticed that certain things seem to irritate your skin? If so, then you probably have Sensitive Skin.

- Is your skin prone to breakouts and blackheads? If so, you might want to opt for a cleanser with acne fighting ingredients.

None of the above? Then you probably have Normal Skin. (And aren't you lucky!)

FINDING SKIN CARE PRODUCTS

Once you've figured out what category your skin type falls into, then you can get skin care to suit—which may seem easier said than done, given the enormous choices available in stores and on-line. But keep things simple! No more than three products are necessary on a daily basis. Remember, consistency is key—you want a cleansing routine you can stick to because it's what you do every day that will make all the difference in the long term.

Start at your local drugstore and look for a gentle cleanser. Avoid those containing abrasives (they'll have the words "scrub" or "exfoliator" on the label) or alcohol. These ingredients are far too rough and drying on teen skin. Your basic skin cleaning tool kit should include:

Facial Cleanser—Obviously, this is your first defense against dirt and oil, the two biggest pore-blockers and creators of break-outs. Look for non-comedogenic and fragrance-free products to minimize irritation.

Light moisturizer (with at least SPF 30 sunscreen)—Make sure to get one that is labeled "non-comedogenic." This will be lighter and less prone to clogging pores. The right moisturizer should leave your skin supple and soft, not oily.

Skincare and makeup products are the largest part of the international cosmetic market.

ADVICE FOR SPECIFIC SKIN TYPES

If you have normal skin, look for a cleanser that exfoliates as well as moisturizes to maintain your complexion's balance.

If you have dry skin, use a cream cleanser that is free from dyes or fragrances, as these can lead to allergic reactions. Avoid any that contain alcohol or common chemicals, like sodium or ammonium lauryl sulfate, as they will only further dry out your skin. Be sure to follow every cleansing by applying a good moisturizer.

If you have oily skin, use products specifically labeled for oily skin. Gel-type cleansers work particularly well here, as they eliminate oil without stripping your skin. Avoid the temptation to wash more than twice a day, as this will only encourage your skin to produce more oil. When you wash, don't scrub, as this will only irritate your skin. Don't skip the moisturizer step either, just make sure to find a lightweight one.

Moisturizer is important, as it will keep your skin looking young and healthy longer and help you to avoid wrinkles.

If you have combination skin, choose a gentle cream, gel, or foam cleanser to help balance out your skin. Use moisturizer on the drier areas of your face, but skip it for the more oily ones in the T-zone.

If you have sensitive skin, it's extra important to look for a label that says "non-comedogenic" or "hypoallergenic." These will be less likely to irritate or cause allergic reactions.

While it's tempting to squeeze a pimple, don't! That's a sure way to create a nice red blotch for your big night out or, worse still, leave you with permanent scarring.

FIGHTING ACNE

If your skin is prone to acne or blackheads, look for a cleanser that contains one of the following ingredients (this is a case where more is not better!):

Benzoyl peroxide: This ingredient kills the bacteria that cause acne, and helps remove excess oil and dead skin cells, all of which can clog pores. You can purchase benzoyl peroxide products in strengths from 2.5 to 10 percent. But be warned, possible side effects include dry skin, scaling, redness, burning and stinging.

Salicylic acid: This ingredient helps prevent pores from becoming clogged. You can buy salicylic acid products in strengths from

0.5 to 5 percent. Salicylic acid is less likely to irritate skin than benzoyl peroxide

Alpha hydroxy acids (AHAs): These are synthetic versions of acids derived from sugar-containing fruits. They treat acne by helping to remove dead skin cells and reducing inflammation. Alpha hydroxy acids also stimulate the growth of new, smoother skin and can help erase acne scars and tighten pores. Be aware that AHAs can irritate skin.

When using any acne-fighting product for the first time, make sure to test it first on a small part of your face (try under your chin.) If after 24 hours your skin seems normal, then you can apply to your entire face.

QUICK GUIDE TO SKIN CARE

1. Consult a dermatologist if you have serious issues such as persistent acne or eczema.
2. Determine your skin type.
3. Develop a routine you can stick to.
4. Wash your face no more than twice a day. Washing more causes your skin to produce even more oil!
5. Use no more than three products at a time.
6. Be gentle! Don't scrub your skin too hard or pop your pimples.

Skin Care regimen

In the morning:

- Wash your face in warm water with a gentle cleanser. Use your fingers, not a washcloth, as this can tempt you to scrub too hard and potentially cause damage to your skin.
- Gently pat your face dry with a clean towel.
- Massage a light moisturizer containing SPF all over your face.

Every night:

- Wash your face with a gentle cleanser.
- Apply moisturizer to dry areas.
- Apply acne spot treatments if necessary.

SPF stands for "Sun Protection Factor," and is your guide to the amount of protection a cosmetic or sunscreen will provide from UVB rays, the type of radiation that can cause sunburn, early aging, and skin cancer.

Be a Savvy Shopper

You probably already know just how much makeup is out there. No matter what kind of store you go to, if they sell makeup you've seen the miles of aisles with what seems like a million different types of powders, creams, glosses and colors. Where to start? What to get?

Take a deep breath. Then start slow and start small. Be organized, be disciplined and figure out what you want before you step into a store.

Make a list and follow it. Don't just blindly fill up a basket with any random product that calls out to you from the shelves. You'll probably just waste your money on some fancy packaging.

Makeup comes in a rainbow of colors. You need to know which colors will look best on you. So, before you buy anything, it's important to determine your skin undertone.

SKIN UNDERTONE: A QUICK ASSESSMENT

Skin undertones are typically classified as either warm, cool, or neutral. A person with warm undertones will have skin that tends to be peachy, yellow, or golden. A person with cool undertones will have skin that leans toward pink, red, or even bluish. A person with neutral undertones will have a mixture of these colors.

Of course, since these are undertones, they are harder to detect than the general color of your skin. A person cannot simply look at herself and know that she has a medium skin tone with red undertones, or a deep skin tone with yellow undertones.

You can get a sense of your undertone by how your skin reacts to sun exposure. If you rarely sunburn, and you tan easily, your skin undertone is likely to be warm or neutral. (African Americans often fit in this category.) If you are prone to sunburn, you might have cool undertones—although

Know that skin undertone remains constant, even as your surface color might change due to sun exposure.

some people with cool undertones do tan well. People with cool skin under-tones often show signs of redness, and may blush easily.

Here is a couple of other assessments that you can use to narrow down what skin undertone you have:

1. Look at the color of the veins on the underside of your wrist:

- Greenish (warm skin tone)
- Blueish or purplish (cool skin tone)
- Can't tell? (neutral skin tone)

2. Get a piece of white paper and hold it next to your face. Looking in the mirror, observe the contrast between the two:

- Does your skin seem yellowish next to the paper? (Warm)
- Does your skin look pink, red or even bluish? (Cool)
- Does your skin seem gray, greenish or yellowish in comparison to the paper? (Neutral)

DID YOU KNOW?

MELANIN IS THE PIGMENT THAT GIVES SKIN ITS COLOR. HIGHER MELANIN LEVELS MEAN WARMER UNDERTONES (THINK AFRICAN-AMERICAN OR INDIAN SKIN TONES.) LOWER MELANIN LEVELS MEAN COOLER UNDERTONES.

WHAT COLORS SHOULD I LOOK FOR?

Now that you've determined your skin tone, pick out makeup colors that will suit your unique complexion. This is a topic that can be very controversial. Some people believe there are hard and fast rules that must never be broken—for example, "redheads can never wear pink," or "blondes shouldn't go near yellows." Take all this advice with a grain of salt, and follow your instincts.

Below are some general suggestions for colors that will likely suit your specific skin tone:

Warm skin tone: Peach, orange, yellow, olive green, dark red.

Cool skin tone: Green, blue, pink, purple, magenta.

Neutral skin tone: You're lucky! You can wear almost every color. Just veer towards the softer shades to avoid overwhelming your complexion.

Actresses Anne Hathaway (top) and Emma Stone (bottom) have cool skin tones.

CELEBRITY TWIN

IS THERE A CELEBRITY OUT THERE THAT YOU RESEMBLE IN SKIN AND HAIR COLOR? IF SO, TAKE A GOOD LOOK AT THE CLOTHES AND LIP COLORS SHE TENDS TO USE. SEE IF THEY LOOK GOOD ON YOU.

Celebrities with warm skin tones include actress Gwyneth Paltrow (left), singer Beyonce (center), and performer Jennifer Lopez (right).

Arming yourself with knowledge of what colors match your skin tones best will not only save you money, but also help you find the right makeup and your best look.

When it comes to skin care and makeup, what's important is what's inside, not the name or the fancy packaging. Look at the ingredients! The best products will avoid things like talc, chemical dyes, binders and preservatives, all of which can irritate skin and encourage breakouts.

In short, where you buy your cosmetics isn't nearly as important as what you buy.

Jennifer Aniston (left) and Kerry Washington (right) are two celebrities who have neutral skin tones.

COSMETICS AND YOUR HEALTH

We want our cosmetic products to be bright, smooth, and long lasting. To achieve this, makeup companies often use toxic chemicals—that's just a fact. And many of the ingredients they use, like phthalates, parabens, sulfates, ureas, and artificial colors (just to name a few), are known to contain carcinogens and hormone disruptors.

Consistent exposure to these chemicals—even in tiny, makeup-sized amounts—can be dangerous to you and your health in the long run. Think twice before you put these on your delicate skin.

To see how much of a toxic chemical can be used before it is harmful to humans, companies often test them out on animals first. Think bunnies, mice, hamsters, chimpanzees, and even dogs. It's an ugly, painful process for the animals and often doesn't really give useful results that translate to humans. Fortunately—mostly due to consumer demand—many manufacturers are working hard to change the raw materials they use, so keep an eye out. You don't need to be a vegan to want to make kinder, healthier decisions when it comes to your makeup!

Some common ingredients used in cosmetics and skin care products are known to cause cancer in humans. However, the U.S. Food and Drug Administration mostly leaves it to the cosmetics companies themselves to decide what chemicals are safe to use in their products. In comparison, the European Union has banned hundreds of chemicals from being used in cosmetics.

Sodium Laureth Sulfate (SLES)

Methylparaben

PEG-40 Sorbitan Diisostearate

EDTA Stearamidopropyl Tetrasodium

Let's Go Shopping

For your first cosmetics shopping spree, let's head on down to the drugstore. First, put together a cosmetic shopping list with the following in mind:

- What colors will look best on me?
- What products are the healthiest for me to use?
- Are cruelty-free cosmetics important to me?
- What is my budget?

Then, list in hand (to avoid buying products you don't really need or want!) start with the following five : Mascara, concealer, BB cream or powder, blush, and lip gloss.

HOW TO CHOOSE AND USE: MASCARA

Mascara comes in black, brown, clear and a rainbow of bright colors. Black is classic and can be used by all but the fairest complexions. Brown is softer, more natural, and best suited for people with light brown, blonde, or red hair.

Clear mascara is subtle and versatile, and makes a great addition to your makeup kit. Use it as a primer for regular mascara, to give your lashes extra volume and shine, or as a topcoat to keep regular mascara from smudging. Also, use it to tame unruly eyebrows!

Colored mascara is a trend that comes and goes. It's generally not for everyday use, but can be fun on wild, dress-up occasions.

Types of Mascara: You'll find a number of different formulas targeted to thicken, lengthen, separate and curl your lashes. Think about how you want your lashes to look—long, thick or curly—then choose the right one for you.

Waterproof or water-resistant?: Go with water-resistant for daily use. While no one likes to look like a raccoon if their mascara rubs off, save the waterproof type for special occasions. You'll need a special remover to get it off properly, and too much use can damage lashes.

How to choose: Black is best to start with. Decide if you want long, curly or thick lashes and pick that formula (steer clear of the formulas that

If you coat your eyelashes evenly with mascara, the tips will be heavy and the lashes will quickly straighten out. To hold a curl, you need to apply a thicker coat of mascara at the root of your lashes and a lighter one toward the ends. One way to accomplish this is by wiggling the mascara wand back and forth at the base to deposit more makeup there, then lightly combing through to the tips.

promise to do everything. They don't.) Last, get a water-resistant type to start with—it's easier to fix mistakes!

How to use: Twist the wand in the tube of mascara to load the brush (never pump! You'll just dry out your tube of mascara.) Wipe off any excess with a tissue or on the edge of the tube to avoid smudges and clumps. Open your eyes wide, place the brush at the base of your lashes (closest to your eyelid) and sweep up. Do this three to five times to get the right amount on. You can also put a light coat on your lower lashes, but be careful not to put too much on or you might see it smudge down your cheeks.

Note: Because you use it so close to your eyes, mascara can be a breeding ground for bacteria. So never share it and toss your tubes every three to six months. Better safe than sorry!

How to Choose and Use: Concealer

Concealers can be used for various needs—think pimples, under-eye circles, and redness. They come in many skin shades and lots of different forms—pencil, cream, liquid, powder—so the key is to determine what you want to use it for and then find it in a shade that perfectly matches your skin tone.

To choose the right concealer, you need to determine what it is that you want to conceal. For pimples, liquid concealers are best. Multitask here and look for one that contains acne-fighting ingredients to help heal the pimple as it covers. Dot on gently with the enclosed wand, your finger, or a cotton swab. Allow to dry, then cover with a light layer of powder so that it will stay concealed all day.

If trying to hide under-eye circles, you can use either liquid or cream. Using your ring finger (because it is the weakest and gentlest) or your middle finger, dot the product softly under the eye in an upside down triangle, then blend.

Concealer can also be used as a light primer on your eyelids to keep your eye shadow stay put. Dot it gently on your eyelid using your fourth finger, then smooth the product into a sheer base.

Gently blend cream concealer under your eyes using your ring or middle finger.

BB and CC creams are found in the makeup section of stores.

BB & CC Creams

BB stands for "Beauty (or Blemish) Balm." It's a supercharged product that's perfect for unpredictable teen skin. Not only does it hydrate (like a tinted moisturizer) and even out your complexion (like a foundation), but BB creams also contain sunscreen, antioxidants, and a host of other skin-improving ingredients.

CC stands for "Color Correcting" or "Color Controlling." It's really just a tinted moisturizer that helps correct issues like redness or sallowness. CC creams generally don't have the skin protecting/improving ingredients contained in BB creams.

How to Choose: Choose the product that addresses the unique needs of your skin, then find the shade that most closely matches your complexion. (Test on your jawbone or neck, not your hands!)

How to Use: Smooth a thin layer over your entire face (as if you're applying moisturizer.) Fingers are fine here, but you can also use a beauty sponge for smoothest coverage.

POWDER

Face powder is great for oily skin, and is also useful for setting concealer. However, apply it with a light touch. Too much will leave your skin looking chalky and dry.

When choosing face powder, pick a shade that closely matches your face color (remember to test the powder on your cheek, jawbone, or neck, not your hands.) If the powder is too dark, you'll just look like you have dirty skin. If the powder is too light, you'll look chalky and scary. Powder is

THE FIVE-MINUTE RULE

At first, don't spend more than five minutes putting on your makeup. You want to leave the house looking polished and fresh, not caked with product. Here's a sample strategy for making you look like yourself, just a tiny bit better:

1. Start with a BB or CC cream for a healthy, even glow.

2. Cover any blemishes or redness with a bit of concealer.

3. Brush some blush over the apples of your cheeks.

4. Curl your eyelashes and apply a coat or two of mascara.

5. Sweep on some lip gloss, and you're done.

meant to look as natural as possible!

There are several different types of powder. Loose powder is best for use at home. You'll need a special brush for this. Twirl it in the powder, tap off the excess and lightly brush onto your face for the lightest, sheerest coverage. Pressed powder is good for when you're on the go. Using the enclosed puff, lightly dab the powder on your T-zone.

Store face powder in a cool, dry place like your bedroom—not in the bathroom. Humidity can cause your face powder to clump together and can affect the coloring as well.

BLUSH

Blush comes in cream, gel, or powder forms. Start with the powder type, as it's easiest to control. You don't want to look like a clown!

Here are some basic color guidelines to help you choose the blush that is right for you:

Fair skin—light pinks, corals or peaches

Medium skin—darker pinks, peaches or mauve

Dark skin—fuchsias, browns and even orangey shades

How to Use: Look at yourself in the mirror and smile. See those cheek "apples"? That's where you want to put your brush. Sweep it up your cheekbone towards your hairline—but don't apply too much! The idea is for a fresh, healthy effect. For best results, you'll probably want to get a special blush brush—the little ones that most blushers come with just don't do the trick.

Avoid over-applying your blush by using a soft, fluffy brush that grabs the color evenly. If you do accidentally put on too much, tone it down by using a clean brush and blending a light layer of loose or pressed powder on top.

LIP GLOSS

Lip gloss comes in clear, tinted and deeply colored shades. Start with the clear or slightly tinted shades. You almost can't go wrong here—any brand will work well! Put gloss on last, after you've done all the rest of your makeup. Then just sweep the wand over your lips and you're done!

Don't forget your eyebrows! They can change the way your entire face looks. Check out one of the hundreds of online tutorials for tips and tricks. Go easy on the tweezing, but do give them some love—with well-groomed brows, you can go minimal with the rest of your makeup.

Tools and Extras

When you feel confident using and wearing your five basic cosmetic items, try experimenting and/or refining your look. Here's when you might want to visit a makeup superstore or the makeup counters at a department store to get some expert advice. But be careful, as they are in the business of selling makeup and can load you up with expensive products and tools. Having a plan before you go, as well as a strict budget, can help you stay out of trouble and find the best products for your needs, as well as the tools that you'll need to apply them properly.

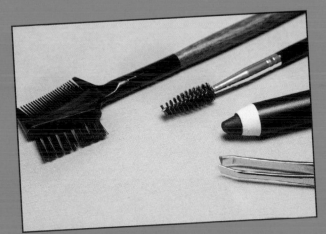

Accessories for care of brows: eyebrow pencil, tweezers, brush, and comb.

BRUSHES

A set of good-quality makeup brushes really can help you apply your make-up with the perfect touch. But be warned, good brushes can be expensive. (Hint: Make gift buying easy for your friends and family when they ask you what you want!)

A good starter kit might include the following:

- Large powder brush.
- Slightly smaller fluffy brush for blush.
- Eye-shadow brush the size of a fingertip.
- Tiny, pointy concealer brush.

NATURAL VS. SYNTHETIC MAKEUP BRUSHES

Natural makeup brushes are made from animal hair—think squirrel, goat, pony, or sable. These brushes tend to be more expensive, as well as slightly more difficult to master. However, brushes made from natural hair are extremely durable, and can last for years with proper care.

Synthetic makeup brushes are made from nylon or other synthetic fibers. These brushes are less expensive, easier to clean, and are just about as effective as brushes made from natural hair.

MAKEUP SPONGES

As with everything makeup-related, these can range from an inexpensive, drugstore brand to a pricey, cult favorite. But using a makeup sponge can make a big difference when applying BB

or CC creams, primer, and foundation. It's probably best to start with the less pricey drugstore versions, and play around with them. Then you can move up the ladder. For the most part, makeup sponges aren't that expensive, so experiment and find out what works best for you.

Smooth, rounded sponges are great for applying makeup to the chin, cheeks, and forehead, while smaller, triangular-shaped sponges are great for smoothing product under your eyes, around your nose, and over blemishes. But be careful! Sponges can give bacteria a friendly home, so rinse them in warm water and mild soap every time you use them and make sure to dry them thoroughly.

How to use: Slightly dampen sponge before use. Put a little bit of product on the sponge and use a dabbing motion to give you the most even coverage. (Don't swipe! Just dab.) When you've covered your face, go back over it with a clean, dry sponge, gently dabbing to smooth and blend everything. Remember, dewy and light is the look you want!

EYELASH CURLER

If you want to wear minimal makeup, this tool can be a lifesaver! Gently curling your lashes gives you that gorgeous, awake look without the bother of mascara. The best part? You'll never have to worry about raccoon eyes.

Even the priciest curler only costs about $20. For the most part they generally all look the same. However, there can be tiny differences in the curve or flatness of the clamps.

How to use: Always use this item before you apply mascara. This will prevent the makeup from gunking up your curler, which can result in damage to your lashes. Insert your upper lashes evenly into the clamp, then gently clamp down on your lashes as close to your eyelid as you can get without pinching yourself. Hold for a count of ten, then release.

ADDITIONAL MAKEUP FOR YOUR KIT

For a flawless, smooth complexion, primer and foundation are your go-to products. Of course, it's a little ironic that at the time you need coverage the most, your skin is most succeptible to irritation and damage from makeup. So, look to formulas that are prepared especially for teen skin

If you choose to wear foundation, you'll probably want to look to the higher-end brands, as they will last longer.

and contain anti-acne ingredients that help heal, soothe, and cover blemished skin.

Primers go on first to prep your skin for foundation. They're meant to smooth things out so your foundation has something to hold on to last all day. For that natural, fresh look, start by using primer alone for the softest, lightest coverage.

When choosing a primer, think about your skin's particular challenges. Is it blemished? Blotchy? Red? Do you have large pores or acne scarring? Keep these things in mind as you search for the perfect formula.

Primer should be applied with the fingers, using a delicate touch!

Foundation is slightly thicker and heavier than BB or CC cream, and provides the most complete coverage available. But use a light touch! The

whole purpose of foundation is to even out skin tone, cover imperfections, and generally polish what you have. Heavy application will look over-done and create more skin problems.

Foundations come in such a variety of shades that you really need to take your time finding the right color match. Here's the gold-standard test: place a tiny sample of the foundation on your jaw line, your nose, and in between your eyebrows. Then go outside and look in a mirror. (Yes, outside into natural sunlight. It really matters!) If the product doesn't blend in, go back inside and try another shade. Foundations also come in gel, stick, powder and liquid form. Liquids are best for teen skin—they give you the sheerest, most natural coverage and are less likely to clog your pores.

If you're not sure which shade of foundation is right for you, swipe them all along your cheek/jawline. If one melds perfectly into your skin tone, you just found the right foundation shade.

DID YOU KNOW?

EVEN COSMETICS LABELED "NON-COMEDOGENIC," "HYPO-ALLERGENIC," OR "ALLERGEN-FREE" CAN IRRITATE YOUR SKIN. ALWAYS DO A PATCH TEST BEFORE APPLYING ANYTHING OVER YOUR WHOLE FACE. YOU CAN'T BE TOO CAREFUL!

How to use: Here's where it can get confusing. If you search for "Best ways to use foundation" you will find scads of sites with articles from professional makeup artists who have all sorts of tricks and tips. Some swear by facial massage before application, others put in a drop of this and a drop of that. For starters, just find the best shade match, and apply it lightly with your fingertips or a sponge.

Take the time to wash your makeup tools monthly! For brushes, it's simple: just fill your bathroom sink with a few inches of warm water and add a couple of drops of baby shampoo or mild dish soap. Swish them around, then rinse until the water flows clear. Dry flat on a towel, as pictured above, to maintain the shape of the brush. Do this regularly and your brushes should last for years.

Where To Get Inspired

So you've bought some makeup, maybe some tools, and played around with them a little. Or perhaps you already wear makeup but want to hone your skills or experiment. Now you're ready for professional advice on how to create the looks you want.

You can, of course, go to a store that specializes in all things cosmetic and consult with a makeup artist there.

Or you can go to the Internet.

There is more information out there than you can review in a lifetime: what to buy, where to buy it, always do this, never do that—everyone, it seems, has a You Tube channel or blog or Instagram account with strong thoughts on what you should do when it comes to buying, applying and wearing makeup. From Jeffree Star to Kylie Jenner, Pixiwoo to Zoella , it's a crazy, ever-changing world of what's hot, what's not, who's in and who's out.

There are a great variety of makeup-related web sites and blogs. Find a few that provide good tips for your particular skin coloring or that fit your personal style.

It can all be super confusing and tempt you into looks that aren't right for you. What to do?

The short answer is, Figure out what information works for you and toss the rest.

What's your Personal Style?

To get a sense of what looks will work for you, you need to have at least a vague idea of what your personal style is.

Take a minute to think about your interests. Are you sporty? Outdoorsy? Quiet? Book-loving? Your style should reflect and celebrate your unique personality. What makes you feel good? What's comfortable? And what feels truest to who you are deep down inside? Be honest—you know when you feel right in your own skin. Trust your instincts and own them. Nothing looks better than confidence!

Get a handle on all this before you wade into the Internet. It's easy to feel pressured to keep up with what's hot even if it doesn't suit you. So be true to who you are and set your own trends!

VIDEO TUTORIALS AND SOCIAL MEDIA

Start by looking for video tutorials that teach you the basics. They can help you master a fresh, natural look and steer you away from common mistakes. You'll be able to tell in a minute or two if the video is right for you.

Keep in mind, though, that videos are often heavily edited, and what looks like someone spending sixty seconds applying a full face of makeup could actually have taken hours! (Check out the bloopers/outtakes many vloggers post. They're both fun and remarkably honest.)

DID YOU KNOW?

THE MOST POPULAR VLOGGERS USUALLY HAVE MAKEUP LINES, SO THEIR VIDEOS ARE OFTEN JUST EXTENDED ADS FOR THEIR PRODUCTS. EVEN SO, IF THEY'RE TEACHING YOU A PARTICULAR TECHNIQUE OR SKILL, AND YOU FIND IT HELPFUL, THERE'S NO HARM IN WATCHING. JUST BE WARY IF THEY PUSH THEIR PRODUCTS AS THE BEST OR THE ONLY ONE THAT WORKS.

Check out social media programs like Instagram and Pinterest for inspiration and up-to-the minute trends. There are people who have Instagram channels or Pinterest boards dedicated to makeup or style. If you find someone who looks like you (for example, has similar skin coloring, eye shape, or style sense), pay careful attention to what they are doing and decide whether it suits you.

DON'T OVERDO IT

We all want to look our best. That's what makeup is all about. But lots of what you'll see on social media is extreme—heavy contouring, harsh lips, overdrawn eyebrows, thick foundation. While it might be fun to play around with these techniques, you really don't want to walk out the door looking like you're wearing a disguise. Makeup should be empowering and confidence building, not a way to hide from the world. Use it to create the healthiest, prettiest version of you!

THE POWER OF THE WEB

When looking for information, try typing specific questions into your web browser, such as "How do I apply mascara?" or "Best CC creams for teens?" The top hits will usually come from fashion magazines, makeup companies, and really popular bloggers. Be aware that, often, the first hits that come up are usually paid advertisements. (You can tell this by the tiny word "ad" you'll see in front of the web address.) While these sites are obviously trying to encourage you to buy a particular item or product line, the information they offer can be very useful.

Internet searches generally present you with the sites that are most often visited, not necessarily the most recently posted or the most useful. So, when searching for information on the Internet, always look at the date of the post or article you read to make sure you're getting the latest information—product lines are constantly changing and trends are fleeting.

There are some great apps out there that can help you choose the perfect shade of foundation, or let you try on makeup virtually, or tell you what chemicals are in your makeup. Again, this is a constantly changing world, so look online for current reviews so you can be sure you're getting an app with the most up-to-date information.

DID YOU KNOW?

SOME POPULAR YOUTUBE CHANNELS FOR MAKEUP AND SKIN CARE INCLUDE: ZOELLA, BETHANY MOTA, MICHELLE PHAN, NIKKIETUTORIALS, PIXIWOO, AND YUYA.

Glossary

abrasive—a rough substance that can be used to smooth and polish.

acne—a skin disorder that usually occurs during adolescence. Hair follicles become clogged with oil and dead skin cells, causing blackheads and pimples to form.

artificial colors—these are synthetic dyes and pigments made in a laboratory. Usually petroleum-based, they can be irritating and cause allergic reactions.

BB cream—also known as "Blemish Balm." An all-in-one facial cosmetic that can be used in place of toner, primer, foundation and sun block.

blackheads—a plug of oil clogging a hair follicle. The oil turns black due to oxidation.

CC cream—also known as "Color Correcting" Cream, CC creams are lighter than BB creams and are specifically formulated to reduce redness and skin discoloration.

carcinogen—any substance that has been shown to cause cancer in humans.

cortisol—commonly referred to as a "stress hormone," it is produced by the human body in response to stress. Too much cortisol can lead to chronic disorders, such as inflammation, acne and many others.

dermal—relating to the skin, or the dermis.

dermatologist—a medical doctor who specializes in skin disorders and care.

eczema—also known as dermatitis, eczema is a catch-all term for a group of diseases that cause redness, flaking and inflammation of the skin surface.

free radicals—molecules that are formed in the body in reaction to bacteria, viruses, pollution, radiation and chemicals. Too many of these molecules can damage other cells in the body. Antioxidants can neutralize free radicals, thus minimizing their effects.

hormone disruptor—these are chemicals that can interfere with hormones in the human body. They are bad news, as their effects can range from cancer to birth defects to fertility problems.

hypoallergenic—describes a product unlikely to irritate or cause an allergic reaction.

melanin—the pigment that gives humans skin, hair, and eye color. The more melanin that skin contains, the darker it is.

non-comedogenic—a product specially formulated not to block pores.

parabens—a chemical that is a known endocrine disruptor, it is very commonly found in cosmetics and skin care products.

pH—an abbreviation for "potential Hydrogen." It is a way to measure the alkaline or acid level of a substance. It's important in skin care because our skin is naturally acidic, with a pH balance of 5 or 6. Many cleansers are alkaline, which can disturb the natural balance. This can cause your skin to work hard to restore its balance, often by producing more oil.

phthalates—another chemical commonly found in cosmetics and skin care products, it is a know carcinogen and endocrine disruptor.

skin type—describes the basic characteristics of your skin. Can range from sensitive to dry, normal to oily.

T-zone—the area of your face starting at your chin, going straight up your nose and including your forehead. So called because it resembles a "T." Usually oilier than the rest of your face because there are more oil producing glands located there.

vlogger—the host of a video blog, or "vlog."

Further Reading

Carmindy. *The 5-Minute Face: The Quick & Easy Makeup Guide for Every Woman*. New York: William Morrow Paperbacks, 2009.

Fornay, Alfred. *Born Beautiful: The African American Teenager's Complete Beauty Guide*. New York: Wiley and Sons, 2001.

Kidd, Jemma. *Make-Up Secrets: Solutions to Every Woman's Beauty Issues and Make-Up Dilemmas*. New York: St. Martin's Press, 2012.

King, Poppy. *The A to Z of Lipstick*. Illus. by David Foote. New York: Atria Books, 2016.

Rayma, Marie. *Make It Up: The Essential Guide to DIY Makeup and Skin Care*. Philadelphia: Running Press, 2016.

Shoket, Ann, and the editors of *Seventeen* Magazine. *Seventeen Ultimate Guide to Beauty: The Best Hair, Skin, Nails, & Makeup Ideas for You*. Philadelphia: Running Press, 2012.

Stanton, Kendra. *500 Eye-Makeup Designs*. Beverly, Mass.: Fair Winds Press, 2014.

Internet Resources

www.mayoclinic.org/diseases-conditions/acne/in-depth/acne-products/art-20045814

An overview of over-the-counter acne products written by the Mayo Clinic

www.safecosmetics.org/get-the-facts/chemicals-of-concern

The Campaign for Safe Cosmetics is a spinoff of the non-profit Breast Cancer fund. Its website discusses the toxic chemicals you might find in your cosmetics and why you should be concerned.

www.davidsuzuki.org/issues/downloads/Dirty-dozen-backgrounder.pdf

The David Suzuki Fund is a non-profit organization dedicated to environmental causes. It provides information on toxic chemicals in cosmetics.

www.peta.org/living/beauty/

What are cruelty-free cosmetics and why should you care? PETA (or People for the Ethical Treatment of Animals) has been at the forefront of the animal-rights movement for decades and offers compelling arguments for making kinder choices.

http://teens.webmd.com/teen-skin-care-tips

General advice article on teen skin care reviewed by a medical doctor.

www.clutchmagonline.com/2014/05/15-bb-and-cc-creams-black-women-should-try/

Clutch is a cutting-edge digital magazine. This is an excellent resource of make-up tips for women of color.

Index

Numbers in **bold italic** refer to captions.